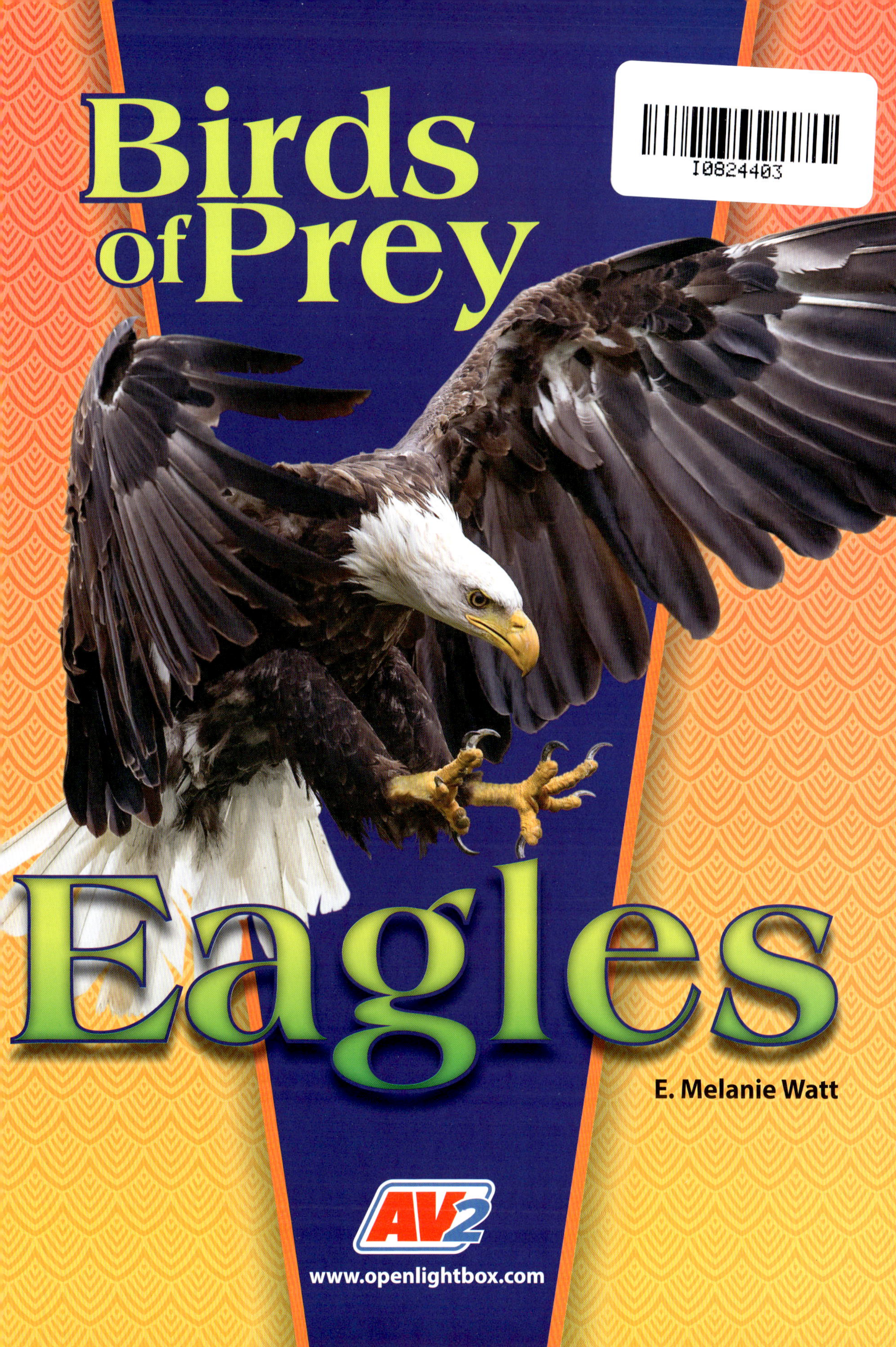

Birds of Prey

Eagles

E. Melanie Watt

AV2

www.openlightbox.com

Step 1
Go to **www.openlightbox.com**

Step 2
Enter this unique code
ZQOCL4W02

Step 3
Explore your interactive eBook!

AV2 is optimized for use on any device

Your interactive eBook comes with...

Contents
Browse a live contents page to easily navigate through resources

Audio
Listen to sections of the book read aloud

Videos
Watch informative video clips

Weblinks
Gain additional information for research

Slideshows
View images and captions

Try This!
Complete activities and hands-on experiments

Key Words
Study vocabulary, and complete a matching word activity

Quizzes
Test your knowledge

Share
Share titles within your Learning Management System (LMS) or Library Circulation System

Citation
Create bibliographical references following the Chicago Manual of Style

This title is part of our AV2 digital subscription

1-Year K–5 Subscription
ISBN 978-1-7911-3320-7

Access hundreds of AV2 titles with our digital subscription.
Sign up for a FREE trial at **www.openlightbox.com/trial**

Birds of Prey

Eagles

CONTENTS

Meet the Eagle.................................... 4
Eagle Features 6
Size and Shape.................................... 8
Eagle Habitats 10
Life Cycle 12
What Do Eagles Eat?............................... 14
Eagles around the World 16
Eagle Encounters 18
Protecting Eagles 20
Eagle Quiz 22
Key Words/Index................................... 23

Meet the Eagle

Eagles belong to a group of birds called raptors, or birds of **prey**. There are many other types of birds of prey, including hawks and owls. Each type of raptor has its own unique traits. For example, eagles are **diurnal**, while owls are **nocturnal**. Typically, eagles are larger than hawks, with heavier bodies and straighter wings.

Eagles have strong legs and feet with sharp **talons**. They also have large, hooked beaks. These birds have excellent vision, allowing them to see prey from great distances.

Cool Facts

Female eagles are usually larger than males.

Types of Eagles

Although all eagle **species** share common features, they have a wide range of different shapes, colors, and sizes.

Bald Eagle

(*Haliaeetus leucocephalus*)

Golden Eagle

(*Aquila chrysaetos*)

Harpy Eagle

(*Harpia harpyja*)

Long-Crested Eagle

(*Lophaetus occipitalis*)

Martial Eagle

(*Polemaetus bellicosus*)

Philippine Eagle

(*Pithecophaga jefferyi*)

Steller's Sea Eagle

(*Haliaeetus pelagicus*)

White-Bellied Sea Eagle

(*Haliaeetus leucogaster*)

Eagle Features

Eagles have many **adaptations** that make them powerful **predators**. One of their most important senses is sight. An eagle's excellent vision is designed for hunting during the day.

Eagles can see prey from a very long distance. They are able to spot a rabbit moving when it is 1 mile (1.6 kilometers) away.

TALONS
Eagles use their powerful talons to catch and carry prey. They also use their talons to carry large sticks to build nests.

EYES
Eagles have large eyes that can take up almost 50 percent of their heads. Their eyesight is four to five times stronger than human eyesight. Eagle eyes are positioned so the birds can see straight ahead and to the side at the same time.

WINGS
An eagle's wing size and shape depends on its **habitat** and hunting style. Eagles that hunt in thick forests have shorter wings that allow them to maneuver around trees and branches.

BEAK
Eagles use their large, strong, hooked beaks to rip and eat their food.

LEGS
Muscular legs help eagles drive their talons into prey to lift and carry it away.

Size and Shape

There are more than 60 bird species considered to be eagles. Although most eagles are large in size, it is difficult to determine which is the largest. Birds are often measured by **wingspan**, but can also be measured by length or weight. For instance, harpy eagles and Philippine eagles can weigh more than 15 pounds (7 kilograms), making them some of the heaviest eagles. However, neither species has the widest wingspan. White-tailed eagles have very large wingspans, but are not as heavy as harpy eagles or Philippine eagles.

With body lengths that can reach more than 3 feet (0.9 meters), Philippine eagles are the longest eagles on Earth.

Eagle Wingspans

Great Nicobar Serpent-Eagle

Wingspan

Between 34 and 38 inches (86 and 96 centimeters)

Lesser Spotted Eagle

Wingspan

Between 58 and 66 inches (147 and 168 cm)

Tawny Eagle

Wingspan

Between 63 and 72 inches (160 and 183 cm)

Golden Eagle

Wingspan

Between 71 and 91 inches (180 and 231 cm)

Bald Eagle

Wingspan

Between 71 and 91 inches (180 and 231 cm)

White-Tailed Eagle

Wingspan

Between 71 and 96 inches (180 and 244 cm)

Eagle Habitats

Eagles live in many different types of habitats around the world, including sea coasts, forests, deserts, mountains, **tundra**, and grasslands. Eagles are also found in many climates. Depending on the species, they may be found in freezing areas near the arctic or in places with warm, **tropical** climates.

Within their habitats, eagles build nests called aeries. Eagles often build aeries in high-up places on cliffs or trees. This allows them to avoid possible threats and easily find food. Much less often, eagles build aeries close to, or even right on, the ground.

Fish-eating eagles, including bald eagles, build their nests overlooking or close to lakes or rivers.

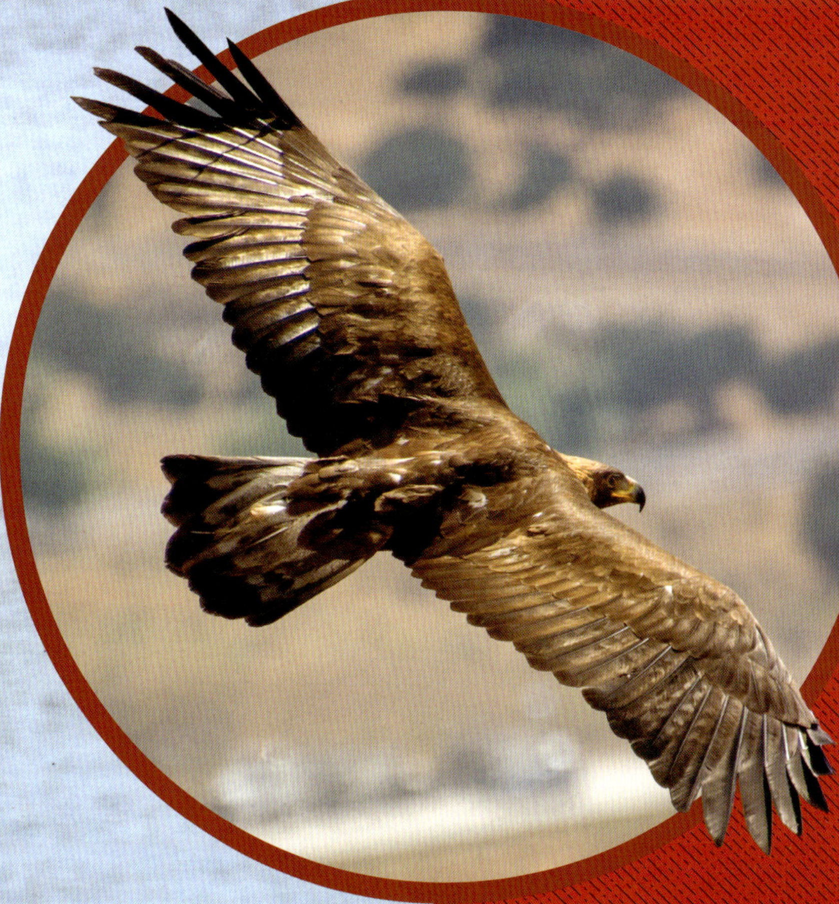

Eagles that live in cold climates, such as some bald eagles and golden eagles, may travel to warmer homes to find food during winter. This movement is known as migration.

Cool Facts

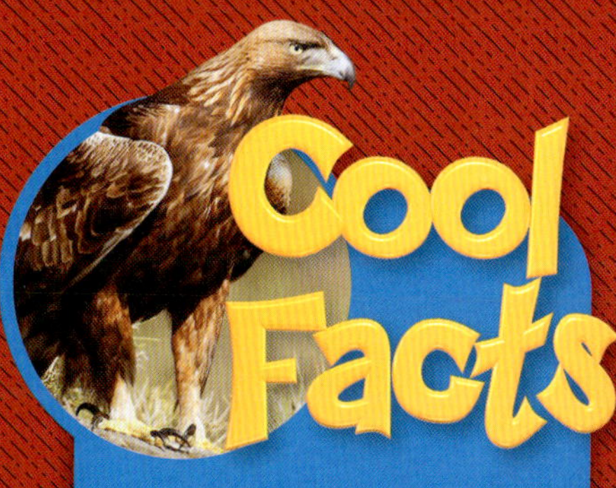

Many eagles add to their aeries every year. A 35-year-old bald eagle aerie in Florida weighed almost 3 tons (2.7 metric tons) when it fell from a tree.

Life Cycle

There are many different behaviors and sounds that eagles use to attract mates. Once they find their mates, pairs often stay together for life. Both males and females help construct an aerie, which may take months to build.

1 Eggs

The number of eggs eagles lay depends on the species. However, most lay one to three at a time. The mated pair both look after the eggs together. One keeps the eggs warm and protects the nest from predators while the other hunts.

2 Eaglets

About five to eight weeks after being laid, the eggs hatch. Baby eagles are called eaglets. They have fluffy feathers known as down. Even as eaglets, eagles have distinctive hooked beaks. Depending on the species, it may take eaglets more than three months to reach their adult size and years before their feathers have the full adult coloring.

3 Adults

Eagles can live a long time. In nature, some bald eagles have lived more than 25 years. Life spans of eagles in **captivity** can be even longer. A captive golden eagle was reported to have lived more than 40 years.

What Do Eagles Eat?

All eagles eat other animals. They often catch their own prey using their beaks and talons. However, eagles may also steal prey from other predators, such as smaller raptors.

Eagles are sometimes grouped into four categories. These are booted eagles, sea eagles, snake eagles, and giant forest eagles. Booted eagles eat many different types of prey. The other three groups have more specialized diets. Sea eagles, or fish eagles, eat mostly fish. Snake eagles eat snakes and other reptiles. Giant forest eagles, also called harpy eagles, prey upon different types of tree-dwelling animals. These can include much larger prey species such as monkeys or sloths.

Sea eagles, such as bald eagles, have spiny scales on their feet. This helps them hold on to the fish they catch.

Golden eagles are a type of booted eagle. These large birds hunt prey in pairs, with one bird grabbing prey that is chased out of hiding by the other.

Eagles around the World

Eagles **breed**, nest, and soar in locations around the world. They eat different types of prey and live in a variety of habitats. Each bird is adapted to survive in its particular home.

GOLDEN EAGLE

Golden eagles live in many different types of habitat in North America, Asia, Europe, and Africa. These include tundras, grasslands, and forests. Golden eagles mostly eat small mammals, such as rabbits and ground squirrels. However, they sometimes hunt larger prey, such as coyotes and young deer.

BALD EAGLE

Bald eagles are the national bird of the United States. Young bald eagles are brown in color, but by five years old have the species' distinctive white head. These birds live in places near water in North America. Flight displays with their life-long mates include clasping each other's feet while flipping and cartwheeling through the air.

HARPY EAGLE

Harpy eagles are some of the heaviest eagles in the world. They are mostly found in tropical forests in South America. Instead of soaring and searching for food, these birds sit still and wait to ambush prey. Their broad wings allow them to fly straight up and attack prey from below. Harpy eagles mate for life. The nesting pair rub their beaks together, chirp, and make other noises to communicate.

STELLER'S SEA EAGLE

Steller's sea eagles are rare birds that live along the seashore or near large rivers in eastern Russia. In winter, they may migrate to coastlines or rivers in Japan, China, and Korea. The same breeding pairs will often build several nests and use different ones in different years. Steller's sea eagles mostly eat salmon, but will eat other prey, including small mammals and crabs.

Eagle Encounters

Eagles can be dangerous to people. Although eagle attacks on humans are not common, they do happen and have resulted in human injuries. However, most of the time, eagles try to avoid people.

People and pets should be kept far away from eagle nests. Even without physical contact, eagles may abandon their eggs, eaglets, or aeries if they are disturbed. Binoculars can allow people to safely view these majestic birds of prey. Eagle webcams have also been set up on various eagle aeries around the world, allowing people to view eaglets and their parents up close, while leaving the birds undisturbed.

Cool Facts

Harpy eagles can have legs as thick as a person's wrist. Their talons are close in size to bear claws.

In the United States, it is against the law to harm or disturb eagles and their aeries.

Protecting Eagles

Eagles are powerful predators, but human activities have placed many species at risk. Threats include hunting and habitat loss from logging or construction. Eagles may be injured or killed if they strike power lines or wind turbines.

Eagle **conservation** programs often include captive breeding, in which young birds are raised in safe places such as zoos. Once they become adults, the birds are released. Eagles are also protected by laws in many places. Some laws make it illegal to hunt or disturb eagles. Others protect important eagle habitats from being destroyed.

In 1918, white-tailed eagles disappeared from the United Kingdom after years of hunting. Today, scientists have successfully reintroduced them to Scotland and the Isle of Wight, off Great Britain's southern coast.

Bald Eagle Case Study

Bald eagles were once common in North America, but by the 1960s, their numbers had dropped dramatically. The birds were being trapped, shot, and poisoned. One of the biggest problems was DDT, a common **pesticide**. This chemical ended up in waterways and contaminated fish that bald eagles ate. When these eagles laid eggs, the DDT in the bird's body weakened the eggshells. This caused many bald eagles eggs to break before they could hatch. In 1972, DDT was banned in both the United States and Canada. Other protections were also put in place, and bald eagle numbers greatly increased. Bald eagles are a conservation success story as they were removed from the **endangered** species list in 2007. Their numbers continue to increase today.

Eagle Conservation Status

Status	Eagle
Least Concern	Sulawesi Serpent-Eagle (*Spilornis rufipectus*)
Near Threatened	
Vulnerable	Steller's Sea Eagle (*Haliaeetus pelagicus*)
Endangered	
Critically Endangered	Philippine Eagle (*Pithecophaga jefferyi*)
Extinct	Haast's Eagle (*Hieraaetus moorei*)

Eagle Quiz

1. What are three ways in which to measure a bird's size?
2. Between male and female eagles, which is typically largest?
3. How many species of eagles are there?
4. How thick can a harpy eagle's leg be?
5. What is the conservation status of the Philippine eagle?
6. How long can a bald eagle live in nature?
7. What is another name for eagle nests?
8. How can someone watch what is happening in an eagle nest without disturbing it?

Answers:
1. Length, weight, and wingspan **2.** Females are usually larger **3.** More than 60 **4.** As thick as a person's wrist **5.** Critically endangered **6.** More than 25 years **7.** Aeries **8.** Watching through binoculars or a webcam

Key Words

adaptations: changes in animals that help them survive in their environment

breed: have young

captivity: not living in a natural habitat

conservation: preserving or protecting something

diurnal: mainly active during the day

endangered: in danger of no longer existing anywhere on Earth

habitat: place in which animals or plants normally live in nature

nocturnal: mainly active at night

pesticide: a poison used to kill animals, such as insects, that eat crops

predators: animals that hunt other animals for food

prey: animals that are hunted by other animals for food

species: a group of animals with the same characteristics; members of a species can usually only breed with other members of that species

talons: sharp claws found on certain birds of prey

tropical: a warm area near the equator

tundra: plains with small plants and frozen ground

wingspan: the width of a bird's wings, from tip to tip, when they are spread out

Index

adaptations 6, 16
aeries 10, 11, 12, 18, 19, 22

bald eagle 5, 9, 10, 11, 13, 15, 16, 21, 22
beaks 4, 6, 7, 13, 14, 17
binoculars 18, 22

DDT 21

eaglets 13, 18
eggs 13, 18, 21

golden eagle 5, 9, 11, 13, 15, 16
Great Nicobar serpent-eagle 9

Haast's eagle 21
harpy eagle 5, 8, 14, 17, 18, 22

lesser spotted eagle 9
long-crested eagle 5

martial eagle 5

Philippine eagle 5, 8, 21, 22
prey 4, 6, 7, 14, 15, 16, 17, 18

scales 15
Steller's sea eagle 5, 17, 21
Sulawesi serpent-eagle 21

talons 4, 6, 7, 14, 18
tawny eagle 9

United States 16, 19, 21

white-bellied sea eagle 5
white-tailed eagle 8, 9, 20
wingspans 8, 9, 22

Get the best of both worlds.

AV2 bridges the gap between print and digital.

The expandable resources toolbar enables quick access to content including **videos**, **audio**, **activities**, **weblinks**, **slideshows**, **quizzes**, and **key words**.

Animated videos make static images come alive.

Resource icons on each page help readers to further **explore key concepts**.

Published by Lightbox Learning Inc.
276 5th Avenue, Suite 704 #917
New York, NY 10001
Website: www.openlightbox.com

Library of Congress Control Number: 2022938854

ISBN 978-1-7911-4712-9 (hardcover)
ISBN 978-1-7911-4713-6 (softcover)
ISBN 978-1-7911-4714-3 (multi-user eBook)

Printed in Guangzhou, China
1 2 3 4 5 6 7 8 9 0 26 25 24 23 22

072022
101121

Project Coordinator: John Willis
Designer: Terry Paulhus

Photo Credits
Every reasonable effort has been made to trace ownership and to obtain permission to reprint copyright material. The publisher would be pleased to have any errors or omissions brought to its attention so that they may be corrected in subsequent printings. The publisher acknowledges Alamy, Bridgeman Images, Minden Pictures, Newscom, Getty Images, Shutterstock, and Wikimedia as its primary image suppliers for this title.

Birds of Prey Eagles

Eagles are sometimes grouped into four different categories. Bald eagles are part of the sea eagle category. Learn more about these birds in *Eagles*, part of the **Birds of Prey** series. Each title in this series explores the features, habitats, and behaviors of a raptor group. Stunning visuals and exciting facts bring the contents of every title to life.

Birds of Prey is a series of AV2 media enhanced books. A unique book code printed on page 2 unlocks your interactive eBook. These books come alive with video, audio, weblinks, slideshows, activities, and much more.

AV2 MEDIA ENHANCED BOOKS IN THE BIRDS OF PREY SERIES

Eagles
978-1-7911-4713-6

Falcons
978-1-7911-4710-5

Hawks
978-1-7911-4707-5

Kites
978-1-7911-4704-4

Owls
978-1-7911-4701-3

Vultures
978-1-7911-4716-7

Follow these steps to access your AV2 book

STEP 1
Find the **code** on **page 2** of this book

STEP 2
Enter the code at **www.openlightbox.com**

STEP 3
Explore your interactive eBook!

OR

SCAN

and enter your book code!

ISBN 978-1-7911-471
9 781791 14713

AV2 is Smart Bo
desktop, laptop,
and tablet frien

View our online catalog at www.openlightbox.com/catalog

Access hundreds of AV2 titles with our digital subscription.
Sign up for a **FREE** subscription trial at **www.openlightbox.com/trial**

AV2 BOOKS ARE ACCREDITED BY  

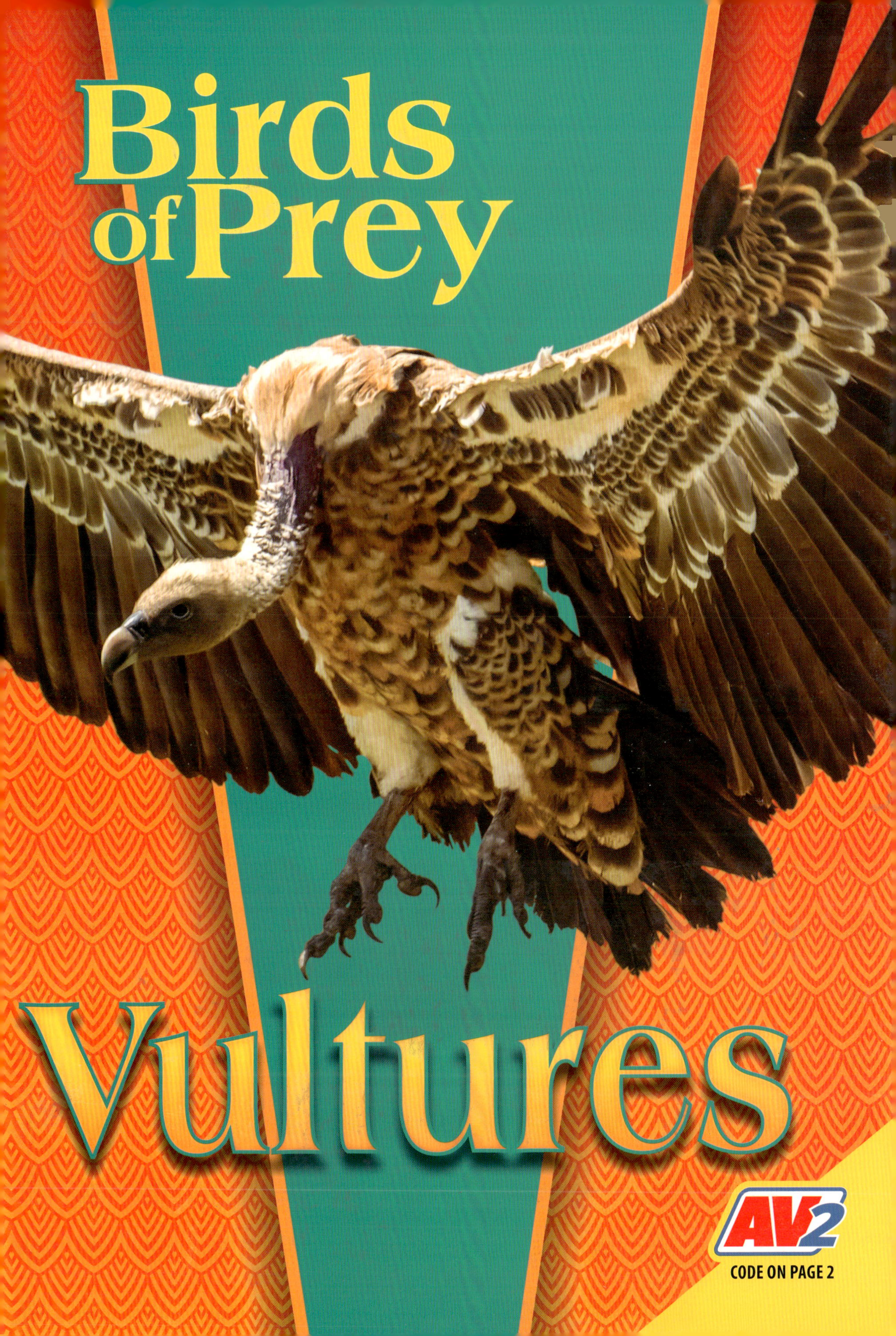
Birds of Prey
Vultures
AV2
CODE ON PAGE 2